Get Financially Fit!

Practical and easy steps to smart money management.

Rio Rivas

Get Financially Fit!
By Rio Rivas

Published by Lulu.com
ISBN 978-1-4357-0810-5

Purchase additional copies of this book at: http://stores.lulu.com/riorivas
Please visit the author web site at www.riorivas.com

Send your success stories, positive feedback, and corrections to riorivas@peak.org.

I dedicate this book to my wife Lisa
and my daughter Sara. Lisa, thank
you for encouraging me to pursue
my passion of helping people succeed
with their personal finances.

Thank you Chuck Orman, you were
the first person to believe in my work.

Contents

Introduction   p.   9

Part One: Define Your Journey

1. Follow your dreams, achieve your goals!   p.   15
    Write down your dreams   p.   16
    Are you financially fit?   p.   17
    What's your *financial step* number?   p.   19
    Identify, clarify, and prioritize your goals   p.   21
    Identify the next action step for each goal   p.   23
    Keep your goals visible and review your goals every week   p.   25

Part Two: Take Care of Your Checkbook and Live within your means.

2. Maintain a Balanced Checkbook   p.   33
    Verify all bank statement charges   p.   34
    Put every charge in your checkbook   p.   34
    Reconcile your checkbook on a regular basis   p.   35
    Do NOT rely on the account balance from the bank   p.   36
    Maintain a cushion in your account to prevent overdrafts   p.   37

3. Live within your means   p. 39
     Use your goals as a motivation to live within your means   p. 40
     Pay as you go   p. 42
     DO NOT borrow money – save up for large purchases   p. 42
     Stop using credit cards   p. 42
     Eliminate impulse purchases   p. 43
     Optimize your expenses relative to your financial goals   p. 44
     Reward yourself – budget weekly fun money   p. 46

4. Eliminate Debt   p. 49
     List your debts in descending order of interest rate   p. 50
     Live within your means   p. 50
     Cut spending and increase income   p. 51
     Establish an emergency fund   p. 51
     Attack the high interest debts first   p. 52
     Make the challenge fun; reward yourself   p. 52
     DO NOT incur consumer debt again   p. 53

Part Three: Invest Wisely

5. Short term savings   p. 50
     Establish an emergency fund   p. 60
     Fully fund your rainy day fund   p. 60
     Invest your rainy day money in a money market fund   p. 61

6. Achieve a Secure Retirement   p. 63
     Invest in the stock market for long-term retirement   p. 64
     Start saving as early as possible for your retirement   p. 65
     Keep investment expenses to a minimum   p. 68
     Aspire to save 15% of your income   p. 72
     Target a 4% withdrawal rate form your nest egg   p. 75

7. Maximize Tax Advantage Savings Plans   p. 77

    Maximize your 401k/403b contribution   p. 78

    Maximize your IRA contribution   p. 79

    How to start your Roth IRA   p. 80

    College savings with a 529 plan   p. 81

8. Retirement Portfolios   p. 83

    Target retirement portfolios   p. 85

    Portfolio 1: Diversified US Index Fund   p. 86

    Portfolio 2: Diversified US and International Index Fund   p. 86

    Portfolio 3: Managed Aggressive Growth Mutual Fund   p. 87

    Portfolio 4: Balanced Equity and Bond Fund   p. 87

    Question: Why invest with the Vanguard Group?   p. 88

Part Four: Real Estate and Estate Planning

9. Home buying and ownership   p. 91
    Be patient and selective in your home choice   p. 92
    Make a significant down payment   p. 94
    Finance with a fixed mortgage   p. 95
    Purchase a home appropriate for you income   p. 95
    Build increasing equity in your house   p. 96

10. Complete your estate plan   p. 99
    Carry adequate life insurance for your survivors   p. 100
    Update your beneficiary information   p. 102
    Complete a will   p. 102
    Complete an advanced directive; assign a healthcare proxy   p. 104
    Give while you are alive   p. 105

    About the Author   p. 107

Introduction

Rio, I just finished reading your publication,
Get Financially Fit! *I needed to have this*
information 50 years ago. I learned the
hard way and it cost me time and money.
It is an excellent guide to smart
Management of money. It is explained
in simple easy to understand language.
–Charles Orman

My mission is to provide you concise and unbiased information so that you can succeed in your personal finances. I challenge you to continuously ask yourself this question, ***what's the next action I can take to improve my personal finances?*** I observe that once individuals decide, commit, and apply continuous improvement, the results are dramatic.

Take a moment and reflect how carmakers improve their product offering. Every year they make small improvements to their cars and every 3 to 5 years they make a more significant model refresh. In the short run it doesn't seem like cars change all that much. But walk into a car museum and look at automobiles from 30, 50, or 70 years ago and you will notice the dramatic difference.

In your personal finance life, commit to continuous improvement and you will experience a dramatic improvement within time. At first, change may be difficult. But in time a few wins will cascade into enthusiasm, and before you know it you will be executing a solid plan and have the confidence to know that you are on track for success. Most importantly you will transform from the pain of believing that you **have to** improve to fulfillment of knowing that you **want to** improve your personal finances.

There are four parts to this book; 1) Define your journey, 2) live within your means and eliminate debt, 3) invest wisely, and 4) real estate and estate planning.

Part One: Define your journey

Live your life purposefully! Identify your dreams and goals. Exercises and tools are provided to help you identify your dreams, assess your financial fitness, and successfully achieve your goals.

Part Two: Live within your means and eliminate debt

There are two key levers to building wealth with your current income. First live within your means. By living on less than you make, you generate money to invest. Secondly, eliminate debt. Debt is like a heavy backpack. As you reduce the weight on your back, you can travel much faster.

Part Three: Invest Wisely

Another lever to build wealth is *investing wisely*. Achieve optimum returns by employing diversified and low cost investments that are appropriate for the investment time horizon. Also know how much you need for retirement and increase your savings until you are saving the right amount.

Part Four: Real Estate and Estate Planning

I recommend that you carefully research your home purchase. You will be well served to buy the right home for your family and minimize the home purchases that you make in your lifetime.

For estate planning, I recommend that you carry the proper level of term life insurance, complete a will, and give while you are alive.

I have made many money mistakes during my working career. For example I have accumulated consumer debt, I have purchased stocks that were in fashion, I have paid high expense ratios on mutual funds, and I have held a concentrated portfolio of just a few investments (instead of a diversified portfolio).

As humans we always have the choice in our outlook to life. We can beat ourselves up or we can accept ourselves and choose to improve. I recommend that you accept the situation that you are in, forgive yourself for any mistakes that you've made to date, and commit to improve. I recommend that you embrace the question, ***What's the next action I can take to improve my personal finances?***

I once heard that the definition of Wisdom is ***skilled living***. While I have made my share of money mistakes, I have also chosen to learn and improve. Over time I have become a valuable resource to my friends and family. My passion pulled me into teaching personal finance classes and publishing a newsletter to help many more people. I am writing and sharing this book so that even more people can win with their money and follows their dreams. I wish you the best success in your journey.

Follow your dreams, and achieve your goals!   -Rio

Part One

Define Your Journey

Financial Steps

 1. Define your goals

2. Live within your means

3. Create an emergency fund

4. Eliminate high interest debt

5. Contribute 10% to retirement savings

6. Pay off credit card and consumer debt.

7. Fully fund your rainy day fund

8. Maximize retirement savings contributions

9. Continuously build equity and pay off
   your mortgage

10. Achieve Retirement Security
    or Financial Independence

14

Chapter 1
Follow your dreams, achieve your goals!

*If you don't know where you are going,
you'll end up somewhere else.*
−Yogi Berra

Once when hiking in a wilderness area, a tired and weary hiker approached me and asked directions to the trailhead. I pulled out my hike book and showed him the trail map. Quickly we identified the route back to his car. He thanked me, and with new energy he hiked off. I felt a great sense of satisfaction helping the hiker get back on course. I then thought, How could he have gotten lost, there are only two turns that he had to make? Later that day as I headed back toward the trailhead it became evident how the hiker missed a key turn. The path to the trailhead was so faint and the main trail was so dominant, you would have guessed it was a game trail. My thought at that point was who would walk in the wilderness without a map?

We all know that we should take a map into the wilderness, but we rarely create and follow a map for our lives. How about you? Are you following your dreams? Are you wandering in the financial wilderness without a plan? Do you have written goals? In this chapter we will identify long-term dreams, assess your financial fitness, outline a roadmap for improving your financial life, and help you set goals.

Let's begin by defining dreams and goals. A dream is an objective that you find highly appealing, but you have not decided and committed to pursue yet. An example of a dream could be to live in a foreign country. A goal is an objective that you have decided and committed to achieve. An example of a personal finance goal could be to eliminate all consumer debt. For the first exercise, we will identify and write down your dreams.

Write down your dreams

To make a great dream come true,
you must first have a great dream.
–Dr Hans Selye

What are your dreams? What would you like to achieve or experience in this life? As humans, we are designed to have passions and dreams. Dreams give us the hope and desire to improve ourselves and help others. Take a moment and write down your dreams using the *Write down your dreams* template on page 28. Note that you don't have to limit your dreams to just financial ones. In my observation, people find this exercise invigorating.

Now that you have written down your dreams, let's transition to personal finance. First let's evaluate our financial fitness.

Are you financially fit?

How do you feel overall about your personal finances? Are you in shape to hike up Mt Retirement? Could you survive in the financial wilderness if you had a setback such as a job loss? I have created a financial fitness survey to help you assess different areas of your personal finance. Please take a minute and complete the financial fitness survey on the next page. The purpose of this survey helps you identify areas both where you are doing well and areas of improvement for your personal finance life. This survey should take less than 5 minutes to complete.

How did you do on the survey? The purpose of the survey is to show you areas where you're doing well and areas where you can improve. If you got good scores (4 or 5) on most of the questions then you are in good shape - congratulations! If you got low scores (1, 2 or 3) on the majority of the questions, don't feel despair. Through focus and continuous improvement you will become financially fit. As you become more financially fit, you will experience less stress and be able to pursue your passions and live your purpose. Later in the chapter we will use the improvement areas to help set your goals.

Financial Fitness Survey

Complimentary electronic form available at www.riorivas.com

	Setting Goals	Poor or No		Fair or Sometimes		Excellent or Yes
1	Honest with myself about problems and opportunities with regard to my personal finance. Open and honest communication with my spouse (if applicable).	1	2	3	4	5
2	Have written short and long term personal finance goals. Regularly identify the next action step for each goal. Celebrate completion of goals.	1	2	3	4	5
3	Organization system for financial paperwork and incoming bills.	1	2	3	4	5
4	Consult with trusted friends to help you achieve success and avoid poor finance decisions. Only purchase investments that you understand and are appropriate for you. Focus on building wealth slowly versus getting rich quick.	1	2	3	4	5
	Checkbook					
5	Verify all transactions for errors	1	2	3	4	5
6	Maintain a balanced checkbook	1	2	3	4	5
	Budgeting & Spending					
7	Live within your means. Know how much it takes to live each month (living expenses). Spend less than you make every month.	1	2	3	4	5
8	Set monthly budget for variable spending categories such as food and entertainment.	1	2	3	4	5
9	Regularly review fixed spending to evaluate reducing household expenses.	1	2	3	4	5
10	Have an established process to prevent impulse purchases (sleep on it, 30 day waiting period, etc)	1	2	3	4	5
11	Research large purchases to insure best value and confidence in the decision.	1	2	3	4	5
12	Set aside money regularly for annual expenses such as insurance, vacation, and Christmas.	1	2	3	4	5
13	Save up for large purchases instead of using credit (autos, furniture, etc)	1	2	3	4	5
	Emergency and Rainy Day Funds					
14	Have an emergency fund equal to one month of living expense.	1	2	3	4	5
15	Have eliminated or have a plan to eliminate consumer debt.	1	2	3	4	5
16	Maintain 3 to 6 months of living expenses in a rainy day fund. Invest the rainy day fund in a secure investment such as a money market or certificates of deposit (CDs)	1	2	3	4	5
	Retirement saving and investing					
17	Know how much I need to save for a secure retirement.	1	2	3	4	5
18	Save enough each month to achieve a secure retirement for your target retirement date.	1	2	3	4	5
19	Review and adjust investment portfolios) annually to achieve desire asset allocation and diversification.	1	2	3	4	5
20	Evaluate and minimize investment expenses. For example employ index funds to achieve market performance.	1	2	3	4	5
	Estate Planning					
21	Have proper levels of insurance (life, medical, etc)	1	2	3	4	5
22	Review insurance policies for both value and competitiveness. Increase insurance deductibles to the highest level that you can afford	1	2	3	4	5
23	Save appropriately for your children's college education.	1	2	3	4	5
24	Have a will to direct your wishes regarding your children and assets.	1	2	3	4	5
25	Purposely give in alignment to your values	1	2	3	4	5

What's your Financial Step Number?

We all desire a s0cure retirement so that we can pursue our interests and passions. Relative to personal finances, I believe an ideal retirement would include no consumer debt, a fully funded rainy day fund (6 to 12 months of living expense), a paid off mortgage, and retirement savings sufficient to provide necessary income for living and medical expenses.

I have outlined *financial steps* to lead you from where you are to retirement security. The *financial steps* navigate you through the financial wilderness. These *financial steps* are listed on the next page. Please evaluate your current status on the road to a secure retirement by evaluating which steps you have completed. Check off all of the steps that you have successfully completed. This activity will take less than 5 minutes to complete.

What step number are you on? Don't be discouraged if you have no or very few steps checked off. I'm amazed at how quickly people advance through the *financial steps* once they become focused.

"I wish I had this information when I started working," is the most common response that I get about the *financial steps*. However young you are, I wish you an expedient journey through the *financial steps* and encourage you to share this knowledge with younger people.

Financial Steps

Electronic version of this form available at www.riorivas.com

Date when
complete

1. Define your goals

Write down your dreams? Identify, clarify, and prioritize your goals. For each goal track the next action that you can complete. Keep your goals visible and review your goals weekly.

2. Live within your means

Pay as you go! Spend less than you make every month. Maintain a balanced checkbook, put your credit cards on sabbatical, eliminate impulse purchases, save up for large purchases, detail your monthly cash flow, and reduce fixed and variable expenses. Achieving your goals is the motivation to reduce your spending.

3. Create an emergency func

Create an emergency fund that is one-quarter of your monthly living expense, then gradually increase to a full month of living expense. Only use the money for true emergencies such as medical expenses and car repairs.

4. Eliminate High Interest Debt

Eliminate all credit card and consumer (i.e. auto loans, student loans, etc) with greater than or equal to 6% interest. Attack outstanding loans with the highest interest rates and lowest remaining balances first.

5. Contribute 10% to retirement savings

Save 10% of your salary for retirement. Use automatic deductions and payments to contribute to your 401K/403B or a Roth IRA. If you can't immediately save 10% of your income then take advantage of any matching available from your employer in your retirement plan. Increase your contributions as you achieve pay increases and decrease payments to service debt. Commit to save for retirement for the long haul. When changing jobs, roll your retirement plan to an IRA - Avoid the temptation to cash out the money.

6. Pay off credit card and consumer debt.

Do not incur any new credit card or consumer debt. Attack and prepay all debt greater than 4% interest. Debts with lower than 4% interest rates can be paid on the regular schedule.

7. Fully fund your rainy day fund

Be prepared for the loss of a job or a serious medical event. Rainy day reserves help make life's difficult transitions manageable. If you're under 30 years old, save 3 months worth of living expense. If you are between 30 to 40 then save 6 months of living expense. Above 40, then accumulate 12 months of living expense.

8. Maximize retirement savings contributions

Fully contibute to your Roth IRAs and 401K/403B plans. Continue increasing the savings rate until you reach 15% of your income. Either invest in index funds to eliminate the risk of underperforming the market and to keep expenses low, or invest in no-load mutual funds that outperform index funds.

9. Continuously Build Equity and then Pay off your mortgage

Purchase a home with 20% down and a fixed 15 or 30 year mortgage. Do not take out home equity line loans. Pay off your mortgage to reduce your living expenses and achieve peace of mind.

10. Achieve Retirement Security (or Financial Independence)

Financial Independence is the point at which your assets provide the necessary income to cover your expenses. You are now in the position to pursue your passions full time. You also can increase your giving.

Identify, clarify and prioritize your goals

Now that you have assessed your financial fitness and determined your *financial step* number, you're ready to begin setting goals. By the end of this exercise you will have identified goals, clarified each goal, prioritized your goals, and identified the next action step for each of your goals.

Begin listing all the goal ideas that are on the top of your mind. For additional ideas take improvement areas from the financial fitness survey (from page 18) and the *Financial Steps*. Your goals can vary in length from short-term goals (less than 1 year) to long-term goals (longer than 5 years). Complete the goal identification exercise using the template on page 29.

Here are examples of goals that I hear from people:
- Create an emergency fund
- Pay off credit card debts
- Get out of debt. Pay off all consumer loans. (Auto, student loans etc)
- Save for a down payment for a house
- Saving up enough money to withstand a layoff or significant setback
- Successfully save for retirement.

Once you have generated your list of goals, you will next clarify your goals and then prioritize them. Clarify each goal by making clear success criteria and a completion date. The goal, 'Increase retirement savings' can be clarified to read, 'Increase Roth IRA contributions from $2000 to $5000 this year.' After you clarify all of your goals, then prioritize them. Assign number 1 to your most important goal. You can identify the top priority goal by asking, if I only achieved one goal, which one would it be? Continue assigning priority to the remaining goals. The following table shows a sample list of goals for a person after brainstorming, clarification, and prioritization.

Example list of goals after brainstorming, clarification, and prioritization.

Priority	Initial brainstorm list of Goals	Clarified goals with clear success criteria and desired completion date.
1	Start a 529 education savings account for my daughter	Open and contribute $1000 to a 529 for my daughter by February.
2	Achieve a secure retirement	Accumulate a retirement nest egg of $1.5 million by the year 2030.
3	Increase retirement savings at work	Increase retirement savings rate at work from 8% to 10% by the end of April
4	Fund a rainy day fund	Increase rainy day fund from 2 months of living expense to 6 months by December
5	Increase retirement savings	Increase Roth IRA contributions from $2000 to $4000 this year.

	Identify the next action step you will take toward accomplishing your goal..	Date Identified
Next Action	Research and identify the 529 plan with the optimum benefits of low expenses, state tax deductibility, and investment options.	01/15

Identify the next action step for each goal.

All our dreams can come true – if
we have the courage to pursue them.
–Walt Disney

Once you have clarified and prioritized your goals, it's time to identify the next action step to take for each goal. It's important to break large goals into bite size pieces to prevent getting overwhelmed. I find it useful to dedicate a single piece of paper for tracking the action steps for each goal. See page 30 for the next action step template. Make a separate copy of this template for each goal. Let's break down the goal of starting and contributing $1000 to a college savings 529-plan account.

Goal: Start a 529 education savings account for my daughter.

Clarified Goal: Open and contribute $1000 to a 529 for my daughter by February.

After you complete action step 1 then immediately identify the next action step.

Here is an example where action step 1 is completed and action step 2 is

identified.

Goal: Start a 529 education savings account for my daughter.

Clarified Goal: Open and contribute $1000 to a 529 for my daughter by

February.

	Identify the next action step you will take toward accomplishing your goal..	Date Identified
Next Action	~~Research and identify the 529 plan with the optimum benefits of low expenses, state tax deductibility, and investment options.~~	~~01/15~~
Next Action	Complete application and send in first $500 contribution.	01/21

I have found that focusing just on the next action step keeps me motivated and

focused.

For convenience and organization, I clip the goal sheet and all of the next action

step sheets (one for each goal) together with a strong paper clip. If you are more

comfortable working on a computer than paper, you can write and track your

goals and action steps in a word processing document or a spreadsheet.

Keep your goals visible and review your goals every week.

Nothing in the world can take the place of persistence. Talent will not; nothing is more common than unsuccessful men with talent. Genius will not; unrewarded genius is almost a proverb. Education will not; the world is full of educated derelicts. Persistence and determination alone are omnipotent.
–Calvin Coolidge

Two important success factors to achieving goals are maintaining priority and persistence. In this section we will review methods for making goals visible and reviewing your goals weekly.

I recommend that you post your goals in a highly visible location. You can put them on in locations such as on your refrigerator door, bathroom mirror, or on the wall next to your computer. I tape my goals to the closet door in the home office. It's important to place your goals in open and visible locations so that you are reminded of them on a regular basis. You don't want to put them in a drawer only to discover them years later when you are moving. In addition to making your goals visible, I also recommend that you also make a colleague of pictures for your goals. This further helps you see your desired future state.

A key to success in any long journey is persistence. I recommend that you review your goal actions sheets at least once a week to keep you focused. Slow steady progress produces significant change over a long period of time. Set aside a time of the week just prior to when you can productively make progress on your goals. I find that Sunday evening works well for me. After playing and relaxing on the weekend, a Sunday evening review of my goals focuses me for the week.

Life Application

I challenge you to create and follow a financial plan. Without a plan you run the risk of getting lost in the financial wilderness. You will succeed when you clearly identify, prioritize, and then persistently work on your goals. Writing down your goals is important because it helps you visualize an ideal future state. You can employ the goal setting process for other areas of your life beyond personal finance. Here are other areas of your life to consider setting goals:

- Health and well being
- Family and friend relationships
- Career and/or business
- Hobbies and interests
- Spiritual
- Personal Growth

Life application:

1. Take the financial fitness survey (page 18) and assess your status on the *financial steps* (page 20)
2. Write down your dreams (use the template on page 28)
3. Identify, clarify, and prioritize your goals (use the template on page 29)
4. Go to work! Focus on accomplishing your next goal – break larger challenges into smaller tasks. Develop action steps for each of your goals (use the template on page 30 for each goal)
5. Review your goals weekly
6. Reward yourself for accomplishing each goal.

Write Down Your Dreams ...

Today's date: _____
Post this page in a visible location like a closet door

What are your dreams? What would you like to do in this life?

Transform each dream from general to specific. Make your dreams specific will make it more clear what you are aiming for and provide motivation.

General example: My dream is to live in Europe.
Specific example: My dream is to live in the Umbria region in Italy for 1 year.

1. _____
2. _____
3. _____

What is the motivation of your dream? Probe this question multiple times until you get to specific underlying answers. This exercise reveals how you are fulfilled.

General example: I want to live in Italy so that I can live in another culture.
Specific answer: I want to live in Italy so that I create great memories for me and my family.

1. _____
2. _____
3. _____

What immediate actions can I take today toward my dreams?

Answer: I can check out books at the library about Umbria.

1. _____
2. _____
3. _____

Goal Setting Template

Complimentary electronic form available at www.riorivas.com

Identify, Clarify, and Prioritize your Goals
1. Identify and write down goals
2. Clarify goals with clear success criteria and target completion date.
3. Prioritize goals. The most important is #1, the second is #2, and so forth.
4. Write down next action for each goal
5. Review this goal sheet weekly
6. When a goal is complete then write down the date, cross off, and celebrate!

Priority	Date Completed	Goal	Clarified goal

Next Action Step Template. (Complete this template for each goal)
Complimentary electronic form available at www.riorivas.com

Identify the Next Action for Goal # _____
Goal: _____
Clarified Goal: _____

Instructions:
   1. Write down goal information from the *goal setting template*.
   2. Write down next action step and the date identified.
   3. Complete action steps that take under 5 minutes to complete.
   4. Cross of the completed action step when complete & then immediately identify the next action step.

	Identify the next action step you will take toward accomplishing your goal.	Date Identified
Next Action		
Next Action		
Next Action		
Next Action		
Next Action		
Next Action		
Next Action		
Next Action		
Next Action		
Next Action		
Next Action		

Part Two

Live Within Your Means
and Eliminate Debt

Financial Steps

1. Define your goals

 2. Live within your means

 3. Create an emergency fund

 4. Eliminate high interest debt

5. Contribute 10% to retirement savings

 6. Pay off credit card and consumer debt.

7. Fully fund your rainy day fund

8. Maximize retirement savings contributions

9. Continuously build equity and pay off
   your mortgage

10. Achieve Retirement Security
    or Financial Independence

Chapter 2
Maintain a Balanced Checkbook

Never spend your money before you have it.
−Thomas Jefferson

To my surprise only a quarter of people who I informally survey, balance their checkbook. For most people, going to the dentist is more fun than balancing their checkbook. Properly maintaining your checkbook is as important to personal finance as a healthy heart is to good health. Keeping your checkbook balanced is foundational for spending less than you make.

Here are five checkbook essentials:

1. Verify all bank statement charges
2. Put every charge in your checkbook
3. Reconcile your checkbook on a regular basis
4. DO NOT rely on the balance from the bank to avoid overdraft charges.
5. Maintain some 'cushion' in your account to prevent overdrafts.

Let's review these points one at a time.

Verify all bank statement charges

First, it is important to verify all bank statement charges. When I informally survey individuals regarding incorrect charges and credits in their checking account, half of the people have experienced checking account errors. The bank is at a significant advantage when it comes to mistakes. You need to identify incorrect transactions within 60 days; in contrast the bank does not have a time limit. If you identify an incorrect charge that happened over 60 days ago, the bank will inform you to contact the merchant who made the erroneous charge.

I wouldn't believe that the banks take such a passive position except that I have experienced this first hand. My credit union incorrectly entered my account for an automatic withdrawal for another client's insurance payment. The bank admitted they made the mistake and quickly refunded the last two payments that were within the last 60 days. But then they informed me I had to contact the insurance company for refunds prior to 60 days. Use your 60-day grace period to identify errors!

Put every charge in your checkbook

In order to keep an accurate checkbook balance it's necessary to log all credits and debits in your checkbook ledger. This means you need to track all transactions including checks, ATM withdrawals, debit charges, automatic withdrawal payments, web payment debits, and deposited monies. The benefits of doing this are (1) you verify all transactions, (2) you see firsthand how you are spending your money, (3) and you know your bank balance. Knowing how you spend your money and knowing your bank account balance enables you to live within your means.

Reconcile your checkbook on a regular basis

One secret to make checkbook balancing simple and rewarding is to balance your checkbook frequently. Balancing a few days of transactions is a breeze – balancing half a month of transactions is arduous. After the initial painful checkbook balancing and reconciling, balance your checkbook daily for the next 60 days. Reward yourself, buy a box of mints and enjoy one every time you balance your checkbook.

Balancing your checkbook daily will only take 5 minutes. You will experience the benefits of both knowing your checking account balance and the satisfaction of being current on your checkbook. You can check for bank balances real time either with web access or telephone banking – gone are the laborious days of reconciling your checkbook register when you receive the monthly bank statement.

Here are some tips to help you with the daily checkbook balancing:
1. Force yourself to enter check, debit, and ATM transactions in your checking account ledger as you make a purchase. Don't leave the store or restaurant before the transactions is added and the balance is calculated.
2. Deduct bills that occur in the current paycheck cycle. For example, if you are paid monthly, deduct automatic payments such as your mortgage, student loans, and car payments right after you

are paid. By subtracting these unavoidable charges early to your checkbook ledger you will reduce the risk of over drafting your account.

3. Establish a weekly time to pay bills. Enter the bills (checks or web payments) at this time. Think, "I haven't finished the process of paying bills until I have entered the charges into my checkbook register."

4. You will quickly learn that you have many more transactions than you expected. You can reduce the number of transactions by budgeting a weekly amount for food and entertainment and then making a single ATM withdrawal. Not only will this simplify your checking account, but also you will have a highly visible process to help you live within your means.

DO NOT rely on the balance from the bank. You run the risk of overdraft charges.

I have seen crises where individuals rely on the current bank balance prior to making a charge. In one case a debit transaction hadn't cleared – shortly there were six overdraft charges at $26 each. Keeping your checkbook balanced daily will put you in full control.

Maintain a 'cushion' in your account to prevent overdrafts.

Maintain extra money in your checking account to reduce the risk of an overdraft. The amount of extra money will depend on the amount of money flowing through your checking account – at a minimum though I recommend always maintaining at least $200. Many banks and credit unions provide free overdraft protection to a savings account. This is a good insurance policy in the event you make an honest mistake.

Life Application

Jump in and do the hard work of reconciling your checkbook. Then balance your checkbook on a daily basis for the next 60 days. By the end of your checkbook boot camp you will be confident and disciplined with regards to your checkbook.

Life Application:

Balance your checkbook for the next 60 days
- Verify all bank statement charges
- Put every charge in your checkbook
- Reconcile your checkbook on a regular basis.
- DO NOT rely on the balance from the bank.
- Maintain some 'cushion' in your account to prevent overdrafts.

Chapter 3
Live within your means

I'm living so far beyond my income that we may
almost be said to be living apart.
–e.e. cummings

Often the most difficult part of climbing a mountain is near the top. Take Mt Everest for example. Between the south summit and the true summit is a steep ridge called the Hillary Step. The challenges include the need to use ropes, exposure to the jet stream winds, and high elevation. In contrast to mountain climbing, the most difficult challenge in the personal finance journey is typically near the beginning. This challenge is *living within your means*. The definition of *living within your means* is spending less that you make every month. *Living within your means* is the most important personal finance challenge that you can take on. Once you *live within your means*, you can accomplish other personal finance goals such as paying off your debts, saving for a large purchases, and saving for retirement.

Here are the essentials to *living within your means*:

1. Use your goals as the motivation to *live within your means*
2. Pay as you go
3. Do NOT borrow money – save up for large purchases
4. Only use credit cards with discipline
5. Eliminate impulse purchases
6. Optimize your expenses relative to your financial goals.
7. Reward yourself - Budget weekly fun money:

Let's review these points one at a time.

Use your goals as the motivation to *live within your means*.

In chapter 1 we reviewed the importance of writing down dreams and setting goals. Identifying both your dreams and goals are important for two key reasons. First it clearly identifies the destinations and milestones on your journey. Without clear destinations we run the risk of being influenced by advertisements and other people's opinions. Secondly, clear dreams and goals act as a counterweight to balance our day-to-day spending. For example, if you are evaluating an impulse purchase you can now weigh the advantage of the potential purchase versus achieving your goals faster.

Imagine that when you are spending money that you are holding a coin. On one side the purchase that you are contemplating is written, and on the other side your immediate goal is written. Shown below is an example where you contemplate going out to dinner and your immediate goal is to contribute to an emergency fund.

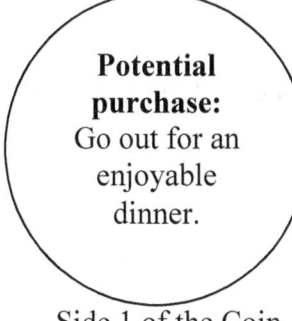

Side 1 of the Coin

Side 2 of the coin

I challenge you to examine every purchase in competition to your immediate goals. You may decide to pursue the purchase (in this case going out for dinner), you may downshift the purchase (in this case go out to a less expensive restaurant), or you may choose to forgo or delay the purchase to achieve your goal faster. The purpose of this activity is to learn to weigh purchases against your immediate goals. In time you will improve your ability to optimize your spending and achieve your goals. For the next week, prior to making a purchase write down both the potential purchase and your immediate competing goal.

Pay as you go

The immediate gratification message that society teaches us is *Play today and pay later*. There has been a steady progression toward more borrowing. Not too long ago that one had to pay fully for an automobile. Today it's quite common for people to finance cars with no money down. In order to *live within your means* you need to *pay as you go*. If you can't pay for something today, then choose to delay gratification.

DO NOT borrow money – save up for large purchases

I challenge you to save up and pay for all purchases with an exception allowed for your home mortgage. Always save up to purchase luxury items such as a television, a couch, a vacation, a boat, a motor home, etc. When you avoid loan payments you decrease your stress and increase your ability to build wealth. Next time you buy a car, save up and pay cash. Save by setting aside the amount of your car payment after your current car is paid for. In time you can transition from buying reliable used cars to new cars that you can drive many years.

Only use credit cards with discipline

Credit cards can prevent you from *living within your means* for several reasons. First the connection between purchasing and the paying is disconnected. When we charge a purchase, the pain of paying for the item is delayed to a future time. Secondly, it is widely known that people spend more when they purchase with credit cards. For example we are more likely to increase our consumption by going to a nicer restaurant or a buying higher-level product. Thirdly, interest payments from credit card balances take money from you every month. If you have credit card balances, I recommend that you send your credit cards on a sabbatical – take them out of your wallet or purse and put them away in a safe place. Pay for all of your purchases with cash, checks, and debit cards. Adopt the practice of *Pay as you go* as opposed to *play today and pay later*.

I think it's fine for people to use credit cards with discipline to take advantage of incentive programs. Spend purposely and pay off the amount due every month. My wife and I currently get back 5% of my purchases toward gasoline. In our case we not only get money back but by using a dedicated card we can track our spending on gasoline.

Eliminate Impulse Purchases

One day I stopped by Costco to pick up some coffee. By the time I made it to the cash register I was holding coffee and two other items. The gentleman ahead of me was carefully pushing his overfilled cart up to the checkout line. As he unloaded items onto the conveyor belt, he looked at me with amazement and asked, "How can you come into Costco and only purchase three items?"

"I only came in for one." I answered. I had a magical moment in life where I clearly saw my impulse purchasing. Wow! I purchased three times the number of items that I had intended.

When my wife and I studied what was preventing us from *living within our means*, we were shocked how 'innocent' impulse purchases can add up quickly. Here are examples of 'innocent' purchases that added together in a single month can have a big impact; Clothes ($20 or more), eating at a nice restaurant ($50 per time), book or music ($20), weekend getaway ($250), etc. My wife and I have adopted a strict definition for impulse purchases. We define an impulse purchase as any purchase above $20 that we have not identified and written down prior to the beginning of the month. We make a list of the purchases that we agree to make such as gifts, car maintenance, travel expenses, etc. Eliminating impulse purchases will help you *live within your means*.

When you shop, go into stores with a list. If you become excited about a new item, add the item to a wish list. On your wish list include the price and the date when you added the item. Take a month to evaluate and research the purchase. The discipline of delaying gratification will help you *live within your means* this month. I often forget to add an item to my wish list by the time I get home. You will learn that fulfillment does not come from buying stuff, but instead comes from appreciating the people and blessings in our lives.

Optimize your expenses relative to your financial goals.

Farmers both prune and thin apple trees to achieve the most abundant crop. Likewise we need to eliminate and reduce some of our expenses to achieve our goals and live our fullest life. Evaluate your spending to optimize your consumption in competition to your financial goals. This is an exercise to identify where you are leaking money.

First identify expenses that can be eliminated. Think of expenses that do not contribute positively to your quality of life. Here list is to get you thinking about expenses that you can eliminate:

- Cancel residential landline telephone service if everyone in the household has a cell phone.
- Stop renting a storage unit.
- Discontinue housekeeping or yard maintenance service
- Sell extra vehicles that require insurance
- Sell the motor home, boat, motorcycle, jet skis etc.
- Eliminate cable or satellite TV.
- Stop newspaper & magazine subscriptions
- Stop health club membership if not fully utilized
- Sell the timeshare

Next identify expenses that can be reduced. Review your expenses and determine where you can reduce expenses. Here you are looking for expenses where a decrease in the level of service will not significantly reduce your quality of life.

- Make coffee at home versus buying at coffee shops.
- Reduce your phone expense by evaluating different plans.
- Reduce the Cable/Satellite TV package.
- Reduce heating expense by running the thermostat 1 degree cooler
- Reduce air conditioning expense by running the thermostat 1 degree warmer
- Reduce internet expense. Change from cable modem to DSL
- Reduce paper delivery only to the weekends.

I am not advocating a lifestyle where all luxuries are eliminated and reduced, but I do believe that spending needs to be weighed against your financial goals. In time you will be easier to identify expenses that do not provide you value compared to meeting your goals. Reducing expenses is an iterative process. From experience, I can warn you that it is possible to reduce spending (and your quality of life) too far.

Reward yourself - Budget weekly fun money:

While it's exciting to pursue and achieve our financial goals it can feel constricting to feel like you can't spend any money. I recommend that you allow yourself (and spouse) a weekly fun money allowance. Pick an amount that won't break the budget (i.e. $10 to $40 per week depending on your income) that gives you the freedom to get an occasional treat, coffee, lunch out, etc. By having a creative outlet it will be easier to forgo and postpone larger purchases.

Life Application

Take on the challenge of *living within your means* every month. If you already *live within your means*, but want to achieve your financial goals faster then take on the challenge of living on less. Identify and address areas where you are leaking money. I also recommend that you employ automatic savings programs (monthly auto payments to your IRA or money market account) – this will help you spend less.

Life Application:

Spend less than you make every month AND optimize your spending and achievement of goals by:
- Use your goals as the motivation to live within your means
- 'Pay as you go'
- DO NOT borrow money – save up for large purchases
- Stop Using Credit Cards
- Eliminate Impulse Purchases
- Optimize your expenses relative to your financial goals.
- Budget weekly fun money

Chapter 4
Eliminate Debt

*Liberty, Sancho, my friend, is one of the most
precious gifts that Heaven has bestowed on mankind.
–Don Quixote*

once went on an Outward Bound backpacking trip. On the first day of the trip
the guides distributed the gear and food such that each of our backpacks weighed
40 pounds. Each day as some people got blisters or became fatigued; the guides
redistributed the weight so that the entire group could travel the fastest. Since I
didn't experience blisters or fatigue, my backpack became a little heavier each
day. Within a week I was a pack mule with a 60 pound pack. The lesson I
learned on this trip was that as the weight of the backpack increased, my speed
and enjoyment of the experience decreased.

In personal finance, having debt is similar to the weight of a backpack. When individuals incur increasing debt it's difficult to achieve goals and stress levels go up. I challenge you to eliminate all of your consumer debt so that you can enjoy life more fully.

Here are the essentials to eliminating debt:

1. List your debts in descending order of interest rate
2. Live within your means
3. Cut spending and increase income to accelerate debt elimination.
4. Establish an emergency fund
5. Attack the high interest debts first
6. Make the challenge fun; reward yourself
7. DO NOT incur consumer debt again

List all of your debts in descending order of interest rate

The first step in eliminating debt is to take inventory of all of your loans, credit card balances, and account balances due. Use the worksheet on page 56 to list all of your debts. Starting with the highest interest rate debt, write down the interest rate, minimum monthly payment, and the total amount due in the first line. Successively add each debt until you have written down all you're your loans, credit card balances, and accounts balances due. Congratulations! You have now successfully defined your goal by writing down all of your debts that you want to eliminate.

Live within your means

Once you have listed your listed you are ready to begin the trek to eliminate debt from your life once and for all. The next step is *living within your means*. *Living within your means* requires that you *pay as you go*. Stop using your credit cards, purposely spend your money each month, and save up for large purchases. all of your debts current by making the minimum payments on time.

Cut spending and increase income to accelerate debt elimination

By living on less than you make you will free up money to reduce debt each month. I recommend that you further increase your available money by both decreasing your living expenses and increasing your income.

Evaluate all of your expenses and determine where you can save money. Can you cut back on eating out? Can you postpone going on vacation? Are you willing to temporarily reduce the quality of your life in order to get out of debt faster? For example, are you willing to turn off cable TV for the next 6 months?

The fastest methods to increase income are to work overtime or take on a part time job. I also recommend that you sell things that you no longer need or that you can't afford. For example, you can sell a luxury items such as an additional car, boat, motor home, or motorcycle. Also consider selling your primary car and purchasing an inexpensive reliable car if your payments are keeping you from getting out of debt.

Establish an emergency fund

Once you are living with your means, you will want to establish an emergency fund. I recommend that you save up 25% of your take home pay so that you are no longer need credit cards for emergencies. This will be $500 to $1000 depending on your income. I recommend that you establish your emergency fund in a separate credit union or bank. Use discipline to only use emergency funds for true emergencies such as an auto repair or medical expense.

Attack the highest interest rate debt first

Once you have set aside your emergency fund then begin attacking your debts. Start first with the highest interest rate debt. Each month make the minimum payments to all of your debts then apply all of your extra money to the debt with the highest interest rate. Once the first debt has been eliminated, then work on the debt with the next highest interest rate. Within a short period of time you will be able to determine the amount of time that it will take to eliminate all of your consumer debts.

When you get to debts with interest rates of 4% or lower, you can go back to making regular scheduled payments on these debts. Say for example, you have an auto loan with a teaser 1.9% rate. I recommend that you not pay off this loan ahead of schedule, instead continue on the *financial steps* journey fully fund your rainy day fund. The rainy day fund which will be invested in money market, certificate of deposits, or I bonds will yield a higher return than 4%.

Make the challenge fun; reward yourself

As you eliminate each debt, reward yourself. Taking a moment to celebrate each success, will invigorate and energize you for your journey. The reward does not need to necessary cost any money. For example, you may take a walk on your favorite path or allow yourself to enjoy a TV show. The reward process is important because while you are attacking your debts you are sacrificing your quality of life.

DO NOT incur consumer debt again

Once you reach the successful milestone of eliminating all of your debts, I challenge you to swear off of all future debt (with the exception of a house purchase). For example, the next time you buy a car, save up and pay cash. Save by setting aside the amount of your car payment after your current car loan has been paid. In time you can transition from buying reliable used cars to new cars that you can drive many years. Always save up to purchase luxury items such as a television, a couch, a vacation, a boat, a motor home, etc. When you avoid loan payments you decrease your stress and increase your ability to build wealth.

People tell me that the largest personal finance challenges are eliminating debt and saving for retirement. The trek to eliminate debt may likely be difficult, but the end result will be rewarding. The key to success is to remain persistent. Once you eliminate all your debt the load on your back will be much lighter.

Life Application:

Eliminate all of your debts:
- List your debts in descending order by interest rate (use the template on page 56)
- Live within your means
- Cut spending and increase income to accelerate debt elimination.
- Establish an emergency fund
- Attack the highest interest rate debt first
- Make the challenge fun; reward yourself
- DO NOT incur consumer debt again

Debt Elimination Worksheet

Date _____

Instructions:
1. Write the debt with the highest interest rate in line 1.
2. Next, write down the debt with the next highest interest rate in each line
3. Repeat step #2 until all of your debts are listed
4. Total up the minimum monthly payment and the balance due
5. Debt elimination strategy:
   - Make all minimum payments to avoid additional charges
   - Focus on paying off the highest interest debt first
   - Aggressively eliminate all debt with the interest rate above 6%.
   - Next focus on knocking off the debts with interest rates from 4% to 6%.
   - Pay off debts with less than 4% on the regular schedule.

Priority	Interest Rate	Minimum monthly payment	Total balance due
1			
2			
3			
4			
5			
6			
7			
8			
9			
10			

Total = _____   Total = _____

Motivational Tip: Reward yourself and family after each debt is eliminated

Part Three

Invest Wisely

Financial Steps

1. Define your goals

2. Live within your means

⟹ 3. Create an emergency fund

4. Eliminate high interest debt

⟹ 5. Contribute 10% to retirement savings

6. Pay off credit card and consumer debt.

⟹ 7. Fully fund your rainy day fund

⟹ 8. Maximize retirement savings contributions

9. Continuously build equity and pay off
   your mortgage

⟹ 10. Achieve Retirement Security
    or Financial Independence

Chapter 5
Short term savings

A penny saved is a penny earned.
–Benjamin Franklin

In the last section of this book we reviewed both how to *live within your means* and how to eliminate debt. In this chapter we will review the topics of rainy day funds and good short term savings options. I recommend that you build a rainy day fund and invest this money in a safe and readily assessable investment. Rainy day funds significantly reduce your stress in life when you encounter one of life's challenges such as unexpected car repairs, a medical issue, or the loss of a job. One benefit of an emergency fund is that it will enable you to stop using credit cards for emergencies.

Here are the essentials to successful short term savings:

1. Establish an emergency fund
2. Fully fund your rainy day account
3. Invest short term savings safely

Establish an Emergency Fund

The process of fully funding a rainy day fund begins by creating an emergency fund. I recommend that you make your emergency fund equal to half a month of living expense. This may range from $500 to $3000 depending on your income and expenses. The important thing is to pick an amount that is appropriate for your household and then work to save up this amount of money.

I recommend that you establish your emergency fund separate from your credit union or bank account to prevent easy access to the money. You may for example start a money market account at a no-load fund family or you may choose to set up a separate savings account at another credit union.

Save up your emergency fund by tightening your spending and living as tight as you can. I recommend that you put your credit cards on sabbatical at this time and carefully map out your spending. Discipline and persistence will enable you to quickly save up your emergency fund. After you have your emergency fund established, then you can continue the *financial steps* (see page 20) by next eliminating high interest debt.

Of course the most important part of an emergency fund is that it is used only for emergencies. A purple leather couch and an airplane ticket to visit a friend, while they may seem important in the moment, do not count as emergencies.

Fully fund your rainy day account

I recommend that you target a rainy day fund size from 3 to 12 months of living expense. Your target size will depend on your age and your career. In general I recommend that if you're under 30 years old, save 3 months of living expense. If you are between 30 and 40 save 6 months of living expense. Above 40 years of age, accumulate 12 months of living expense. You should increase these amounts if you are in a career that requires a long time to get hired. Conversely you can reduce your rainy day target balance if you are confident that you can quickly land a job in the event that you lose yours.

Before you go to work funding your rainy day fund, I think it's best to eliminate some of your consumer debts and start your retirement savings. Refer to the *financial steps* on page 20. I recommend eliminating debts with interest rates greater than 4% since these loans cost you more than you can make in short term savings. Next, save target 10% of your income in your retirement savings plan at work or with an IRA while accumulating your rainy day fund. If you can't afford the full 10%, then at least save in your retirement savings plan to achieve all of the matching contributions from your employer. I think it's important to start the retirement savings as early as possible since both the early contributions and the savings habits are key success factors for retirement success.

Invest your rainy day money in a money market fund

The investment objectives of your rainy day fund are safety, liquidity, and returns that are great than inflation over the long run. Safety refers to taking low risk such that your principal investment does not decrease. Liquidity is the ability to gain access to the money in the event that you need it. Savings accounts at banks and credit unions provide safety and liquidity, but almost always pay low rates of interest. Bank certificates of deposit (CDs) insured by FDIC and treasury bills are safe investments and provide good returns, but do not provide the desired liquidity. Stock mutual funds are liquid but have highly volatile returns in the short term. Overall I think that the best overall investment for a rainy day fund is a high quality money market investment. Let's examine money market funds in more detail.

Money market funds provide very good liquidity and good returns relative to savings accounts. Money market funds typically invest in short term government bonds, short-term financial institution notes, and short-term corporate bonds. Most money market accounts incorporate a checking account to provide immediate access to funds. I recommend that you choose a money market fund with low expenses. Here are historic returns for two low cast money market funds:

Money Market (January 2008) Fund	Compound yield	5 Year Return	Expense Ratio	Minimum Investment
Vanguard Prime Market Fund (#30)	4.58%	2.99%	0.24%	$3,000
Fidelity Money Market (#454)	4.76%	2.94%	0.42%	$25,000

The web sites for these money market funds are www.vanguard.com and www.fidelity.com.

Money market example: John and Mary are married and in their late 30's. They have accumulated $24,000 for their rainy day account. For them this is 6 month of living expense ($4000 per month). Switching $24,000 from a savings account (0.6% interest) to a money market account (4.6%) increases investment returns from $144 to $1100 for the year. If they need money quickly they can transfer funds by completing an electronic transfer to their checking account or by writing a check.

Chapter 5
Achieve a Secure Retirement

Resolve never to be poor,
Whatever you earn, spend less.
–Samuel Johnson

What's your vision of an ideal retirement? Is it spending more time with friends and family, using your talents to help other people, or working tediously to lower your golf score? Whatever your dreams are, it's important to make sure that you are on the road to a financially secure retirement. How well are you doing on your retirement savings and planning? Do you know how much you need for a secure retirement? Do you know if you are saving enough? Unfortunately gone are the days when employees could count on social security and pensions to provide a sound retirement. We need to step forward and take responsibility for our own retirement security. From wherever you are, there are changes and improvements that you can make to improve your retirement. Here are the essentials to build a secure retirement.

1. Invest in the stock market for long-term retirement needs
2. Start saving as early as possible
3. Keep investment expenses to a minimum
4. Aspire to save 15% of your income toward retirement.
5. Target a 4% withdrawal rate from nest egg in retirement

Let's review these points one at a time.

Invest in the stock market for long-term retirement savings.

There are a wide variety of investment vehicles available to build your retirement nest egg. The table shows the growth of a $10,000 in treasury bills, bonds, and the stock market investments using historical returns.

Historical growth of $10,000 Based on 30 Year Historical Returns

Vehicle	Inflation	Treasury Bills	Bonds		Stock Market
Portfolio		Risk free	Conservative	Balanced	Growth
Starting Balance	$10,000	$10,000	$10,000	$10,000	$10,000
Historical Return	3.2%	3.8%	5.4%	8.0%	12.0%
10 years	$13,702	$14,520	$16,920	$21,589	$31,058
20 years	$18,776	$21,084	$28,629	$46,610	$96,463
30 years	$25,727	$30,614	$48,442	$100,627	$299,599

The table illustrates how a higher rate of return investment makes a significant difference over time. The initial $10,000 investment grew to $21,084 in treasury bills, but grew to $96,463 in the stock market over a 20-year period! Over the long-term, the stock market has yielded higher returns than either treasury bills or bonds, but in the short term the stock market is more volatile. This illustrates why investing in the stock market is appropriate for a long-term goal such as retirement. As one nears retirement it's prudent to adjust the asset allocation to 50% stocks and 50% bonds.

Here is the formula to calculate the future value of an investment based on the number of years and the expected rate of return:

$$\text{Future Value} = \text{Present Value} \times (1 + \text{rate of return})^{\text{Years}}$$
$$\text{Future Value} = \$10{,}000 \times (1 + 0.12)^{20} = \$96{,}463$$

The exponential math is the reason that increasing time and increasing the rate of return make such a big difference to the future value. Many people refer to the power of compounding returns as the eighth wonder of the world.

Start Saving as Early as Possible for your Retirement

Imagine two different investors; person A saves $100 per month for the next seven years and then saves nothing between years 8 and 30. Person B saves nothing for the next seven years, but then saves $100 per month between years 8 and 30. Person A saves a total of $8400 and person B saves $27,600. **Who will have the most money in 30 years assuming a 12% rate of return in the stock market?**

If you guessed that person A accumulated the most money, you are correct! The table below shows the accumulated total savings for person A, person B, and person C who invest $100 per month for all 30 years.

The Impact of Saving $100 per Month

Person	Early A	Delay B	Consistent C
Starting Balance	$0	$0	$0
Years 1-7	$100 per month	$0 per month	$100 per month
Years 8-14	$0 per month	$100 per month	$100 per month
Years 15-21	$0 per month	$100 per month	$100 per month
Years 22-30	$0 per month	$100 per month	$100 per month
Total saved	$8,400	$27,600	$36,000
Expected rate of return	12.0%	12.0%	12.0%
7 years	**$12,100**	**$0**	**$12,100**
14 years	**$26,750**	**$12,100**	**$38,850**
21 years	**$59,100**	**$38,800**	**$98,000**
30 years	**$164,000**	**$125,500**	**$289,500**

How can person A have more money when they have invested less than one-third the amount of money of person B? The answer is that by the end of 7 years, person A's investment nest egg of $12,100 will has an expected return of $1440[1], which is more than return more than person B's year 8 contribution of $1200[2]. The takeaway from this exercise is that **the amount that you invest during the next 7 years will account for half of your retirement savings.** I recommend that either start or increase your retirement savings as much as you can today. A valid exception to postpone retirement savings is if you are continuing your education to improve your income potential.

What happens if person C invests $100 per month for the whole 30-year period? The answer is easy – Person C's nest egg is simply the sum of person A and person B's nest egg. Notice that every $100 per month contribution in the stock market grew to almost $300,000. This means that somebody saving $400 per month would accumulate more than a million dollars over a 30 year period.

---

[1] $12,000 nest egg x 12% rate of return = $1440 expected return
[2] $100 per month x 12 months = $1200 contribution

Keep investment expenses to a minimum.

When investing, the majority of people don't evaluate the significant impact of investment expenses over time. There are three types of mutual funds relative to expenses; index funds, no-load managed mutual funds, and loaded mutual funds.

Index funds are designed to mirror major market indices such as the Wilshire 5000 (the largest 5000 US Corporations) or the S&P 500 (the largest 500 US corporations). The most common index that you hear quoted daily is the Dow Jones Industrial (which tracks 30 large Corporations).

One key feature of an index funds is that the ownership of different shares is proportion to the market value of each corporation. This is to say that the Wilshire 5000 index invests a lot more in large corporations such as Exxon and Microsoft, and a lot less in a small growing company such as Starbucks. Index funds are self-correcting in that they will increase investments in winning companies like Microsoft and Starbucks and divest from tanking companies such as and Enron and WorldCom. Given that these adjustments occur daily, an index fund investor can sleep soundly knowing that they don't have to worry about the performance of individual stocks.

The most significant advantage of index fund investing is the low expense ratio fee. The average managed mutual fund has an annual expense ratio of 1.35%, while index fund expense ratios from low cost mutual fund companies such as Vanguard and Fidelity are 0.2%. This represents a 6X reduction in cost from the typical mutual fund– this is like buying a $30,000 car for just $5,000.

Managed mutual funds differ from index funds in that the fund manager attempts to beat the index by picking a portfolio of stocks. In the long-term, less than 20% of managed funds outperform index funds; therefore the risk with managed funds is that 80% of the time you will end up with lower performance plus higher expenses. Average expense on a no-load managed fund is 1.35%, but can range from 0.4 to 2% depending on the specific fund. I recommend that you only purchase managed funds that have outperformed their comparative index for last 3, 5, and 10 years.

Loaded mutual funds charge an upfront sales fee of 3% to 6% and have annual expenses that range from 1 to 2%. The upfront sales fee is charged to provide a commission to the salesperson. For example, a 5% load fee means that only $95 out of every $100 is invested. I recommend that you NEVER invest in loaded mutual funds since a portion of your money is confiscated. The graph below shows the impact of expenses when investing $100 per month over 30 years.

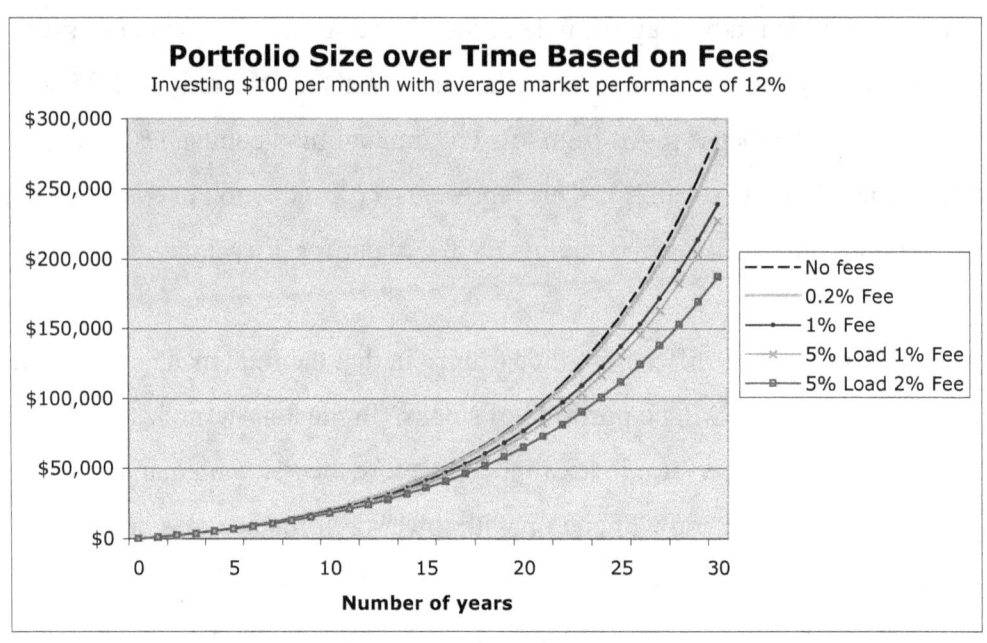

Portfolio Size over Time Based on Fees

Investing $100 per month with average market performance of 12%

Legend:
- – – – No fees
- 0.2% Fee
- 1% Fee
- 5% Load 1% Fee
- 5% Load 2% Fee

Number of years

In this calculation different levels of fees are applied to average annual historic stock market return of 12%. In reality the returns for different mutual funds vary and 80% of managed funds do not achieve average market performance. The black dashed line represents a portfolio without fees.

The impact of expected returns based on the expense ratios and upfront fees is quite dramatic. Examine the difference in the expected return at 30 years of each portfolio versus the benchmark index. The expenses of an index fund only absorb 4% of the portfolio potential, while the expenses of a loaded fund confiscates 35% of your portfolio potential. A mutual fund with a 1% expense ratio eats into 17% of your portfolio. Many investors do not notice the impact of fees until their portfolios are large. I recommend that you think with the end portfolio in mind. Employ low fee mutual funds all of the time to maximize your nest egg.

While the popularity of index funds is increasing, there are two reasons why most people invest in mutual funds. First investors don't notice the impact of the expenses. Second, the mutual fund industry has effectively marketed its products as outperforming relative indexes.

The ability of expense ratios to erode your portfolio is the best-kept investment secret on the planet. Imagine that we lived in a world where the expense ratio is charge after 30 years of investing, just as you retire. You and I would jump, scream, and throw a tantrum if we lost 17% to 35% of our portfolio on the last day. Most people have not seen the math of expense ratios, and thus they do not see that their portfolio is leaking. People I advise become angry when they learn that 'investment advisers' have sold them expensive loaded funds. Once they understand the impact of expense ratios they fire the 'investment adviser' and roll their funds to an index fund.

Another reason that people don't scrutinize expense ratios is because mutual funds have effectively marketed their products as being better than index funds. Pick up an investment magazine and you will find many advertisements showing mutual funds that have beat their benchmark index. Now pick up an investment magazine several years later and you will observe that the mutual funds change the funds in their advertisements based on historic performance. Mutual fund companies showcase their current best performing mutual fund in order to put their best image forward.

Aspire to save 15% of your income

There are two approaches to retirement savings. One approach is to determine the desired retirement income and then back calculate the required savings nest egg. A second approach is to maximize retirement savings and attempt to achieve retirement security and financial independence as early as possible. Financial independence is the point at which your investment incomes are equal to or greater than your living expenses.

Your retirement income stream will be based on social security savings, a pension if applicable, and the size of the retirement nest egg that you accumulate. The department of social security sends out regular estimates of your social security income. If you are eligible for a pension, your benefits department can provide an income estimate. Once you determine the income shortfall, you can determine your required nest egg from retirement calculators at web sites such as Vanguard.com, TIAA-CREF.com, and Fidelity.com. I recommend that you estimate your required nest egg using multiple retirement calculators.

The table below shows the expected size of the retirement nest egg (measured in multiples of your salary) versus the percent of salary saved and the number of years of savings.

Retirement Savings in Multiples of Annual Salary

	Percent of Income Saved		
Years	5%	10%	15%
5	0.3	0.6	1.0
10	0.9	1.8	2.6
15	1.9	3.7	5.6
20	3.6	7.2	9.5
25	6.7	13.3	20.0
30	12.0	24.1	36.2
35	21.6	38.4	64.8
40	38.4	76.7	115.0

The table shows the importance of saving over a long period of time and saving the highest percent of your salary that you can afford. Notice in this table that every increase in 5% savings rate translates into reaching the same salary multiple approximately 5 years earlier. Overall the number of years to save is determined by our current age and target retirement age. Our ability to save is determined by our intention, motivation and discipline – we have to make the difficult tradeoff of today's quality of life versus tomorrow's quality of life.

The chart below shows the expected retirement income (measured in percent of your salary) as a function of the percent salary saved and the number of years of savings. To achieve financial independence target 100% of your current salary.

Retirement Income in Percent of Current Annual Salary

Years	Percent of Income Saved		
	5%	10%	15%
5	1%	2%	4%
10	4%	7%	10%
15	8%	15%	22%
20	14%	29%	38%
25	27%	53%	80%
30	48%	96%	145%
35	86%	154%	259%
40	154%	307%	460%

Notice how starting early (more years) and increasing contributions significantly increases the amount saved. This is why I recommend that people begin saving as early as possible and save 15% of their income. There super savers who are called extreme savers. These people save over half of their income by living simply and giving up today's quality of life for the future. You can become an extreme saver by living off every other paycheck. Extreme savers achieve financial independence in less than 20 years. For a person saving 50%, multiply the 10% column in the table above by 5 to determine the percent of current income.

Target a 4% withdrawal rate from your nest egg

How much can you withdraw from your nest egg when you are in retirement? With a balanced portfolio of 50% stocks and 50% bonds, statistical math calculations reveal that 4% of a portfolio can be safely withdrawn without eroding the size of the portfolio. In the field of mathematics is a statistical method called Monte Carlo Simulation (named after the gambling city in Europe). Monte Carlo simulation involves completing calculations for many probable scenarios to help in decision-making. In the example of withdrawing money out of a retirement account the key parameters are the percent of the portfolio withdrawn each year and historical stock and bond market returns. Through calculation of over a hundred of scenarios, the success rate of your retirement plan can be evaluated.

A web site that explains this concept in more detail and provides both a calculator (Called FIRECalc) to predict how long you can survive off of your nest egg is: www.fireseeker.com. I recommend that you run the calculator multiple times to see how your annual spending, nest egg size, percentage of portfolio in stock, and expense ratios impact how long your money will last. These calculations are based on inflation and a balanced portfolio of 50% stocks and 50% bonds (see chapter 6 for an example of a balanced portfolio). In practical terms this means that every $100,000 in retirement savings, provides an annual income of $4,000.

Life Application

Now is the time to make improvements to your retirement plan and strategy. For some people it's jumping in and starting a 401k or 403b to the level of employer matching. For other people it's increasing the rate of savings. Yet for others it may be a major remodeling effort to roll over your 401k/403b or IRA to a low cost no-load mutual fund family. The one thing I find is that everyone can readily identify his or her next hurdle and challenge. Identify your improvements, commit to complete them, and have the courage to take the next steps.

Life Application:

Get your retirement plan in order:
- Invest in the stock market for long-term retirement needs.
- Start saving as early as possible
- Keep investment expenses to a minimum
- Aspire to save 15% of your income.
- Target a 4% withdrawal from your nest egg in retirement.

Chapter 6
Maximize Tax Advantaged Savings Plans

*One man pretends to be rich yet
has nothing, and another pretends
to be poor yet has great wealth.
-Proverbs 13:7*

Today when Americans identify their most significant asset, it's their house. Within a few decades I believe we will identify our retirement nest egg as our largest assets. I think this is a great shift since we will need large nest eggs for retirement security.

Tax advantaged savings plans such as 410k/403b plans and IRAs have significantly improved in the last decade. The latest updates not only include much higher contribution levels, but also contributions limits that are indexed to inflation. I recommend that you optimize your contributions both to achieve retirement security and your daily quality of life. Here are the essentials to tax advantaged savings.

1. Maximize your 401K/403b contribution
2. Maximize your IRA contribution
3. How to start your Roth IRA
4. College savings with a 529 plan

Let's review these points one at a time.

Maximize your 401K/403b contribution.

Corporations typically provide 401K programs, while non-profit institutions typically provide 403b programs. The benefit of these programs is that you get to save money and delay paying tax. When you make the contributions you are not taxed on the money, the money grows tax free, and then you pay tax when you withdraw the money in retirement. Employers provide matching contributions in many 401K and 403b plans. You should always take advantage of the matching contribution. Ideally your 401K or 403b program has no-load (no sales charges) investment options and low expense ratios (less than 1%, lower is better).

The maximum allowable contribution for 410k/403b plans in 2008 is $15,500 for individuals under 50. Individuals over 50 are allowed an additional $5000 catch-up contribution. The maximum allowable contributions beyond 2008 are indexed to inflation. Check with your human resources department for the current maximum contributions. I recommend that you maximize your contribution to your plan.

Many companies now offer an option called a Roth 401K. With this plan your contributions are made after you pay tax, your money grows tax free and you are NOT taxed when you withdraw money in retirement (since you have already paid tax). The question people ask is, Should I contribute some or all my money into a

Roth 401K? I believe that the benefits of a Roth 401K are highest for those who 1) can easily maximize both their 401k and IRA contributions, 2) anticipate higher tax rates in retirement (therefore pay today at lower tax rates), and 3) desire to pass money to descendants in the most tax advantaged manner.

Maximize your IRA contribution.

There are two types or IRAs, Roth and traditional. The recommended IRA for new investments is the Roth IRA due to the long-term tax advantages. Of course if you exceed the income limitations then a traditional IRA is the next best option. The traditional IRA is used when rolling a 401K or 403b plan from your employer. I recommend setting up automatic monthly withdrawals from your checking account for discipline. The table below details the difference between the Roth and traditional IRA.

	Roth IRA	**Traditional**
Maximum contribution (Catch up provision for individuals over 50)	2008: $5000 **$416.66 / month** ($6000 if over 50)	2008: $5000 **$416.66 / month** ($6000 if over 50)
"Phase-out" income Limits. Full contribution allowed at lower limit. Prorated contribution between the limits.	Single AGI $101,000 to $116,000. Married AGI $159,000 to $169,000.	No income limits to contribute. (Tax deductability is single AGI $53,000. Married AGI $83,000)
Tax Consequences	After tax money used. Money grows tax free. Never taxed again!	Pre-tax money used. Money grows tax free. Taxed upon withdrawal.
Comment	Recommended for new investments due to tax advantages	Practical account to rollover retirement accounts

How to Start Your Roth IRA.

A Roth IRA is a great retirement savings vehicle. Monies are invested with after tax dollars and grow tax-free. When you withdraw your money in retirement you will not pay taxes Let's review income limits, contribution limits, and the easiest way to get started.

Individuals are allowed to invest $5000 in 2008 (if you are over 50, you can add an additional $1000) as long as their adjusted gross income is less than $101,000. The adjusted gross income is shown on line 4 on a 1040EZ tax form, it's on the bottom of page 1 for a regular 1040 form. If you make between $101,000 and $116,000 the allowed contribution is gradually phased out. Above an adjusted gross income of $116,000 a Roth IRA contribution is not allowed. A married couple can invest $5000 each as long as the combined adjusted gross income is less than $159,000. Above an adjusted gross income of $169,000 the allowed contribution is phased out. If you exceed these income limits then you can invest in a traditional IRA.

Starting a Roth IRA is easy. Simply contact a no-load mutual fund company by telephone or visit their web site. Today one can complete the Roth IRA application on-line. A great investment option for starting your Roth IRA is a target retirement fund. Once you identify the year (rounded to the nearest 5) that you want to retire you have selected your fund. For example if you want to retire in 2033, you would go with the 2035 target retirement fund. Target retirement funds automatically transitions from a high percentage of stock market investments to a balance of stocks and bonds.

College savings with a 529 plan

Before you fund your children's education accounts, it's important to make sure that you are saving adequately for your own retirement. It's critical to not delay your own retirement savings because time is a critical success factor when investing.

Congress passed a law requiring all states to offer 529 plans. A 529 plan allows you to save money for your child's college education with tax advantages similar to a Roth IRA. You contribute after tax money and then it grows tax-free. You can invest in a 529 plan in any state plan, but it's important to weigh both the advantages of the in state program and expenses. If you live in a state without state income tax then consider the Utah plan. If you live in a state with state income tax then it's worthwhile to see how much your contribution may be state tax deductible. Overall go with a plan that has no-load funds and low expenses.

The limits on contributions are quite high – you can contribute up to $60,000 per child per year for a total of $250,000 over the duration of the savings plan. If your child does not use the funds for college you can maintain the same beneficiary for future education, change the beneficiary, or redeem funds by paying tax on the gains plus a 10% penalty.

Chapter 7
Retirement Portfolios

He who tends a fig tree will eat its fruit.
                                                -Proverbs 27:18

The table below provides an overview of 5 different investment portfolios. The portfolios are designed to have low expense ratios to maximize the return to you. The expense ratio (annual cost per year) is less than 0.4% for all portfolios. In contrast the average expense ratio in the mutual fund industry is 1.35%.

Portfolio	Best for...	Upkeep	Expense Ratio
Target Retirement	Person who wants seeks the easiest investment strategy. Investment automatically becomes more conservative over time.	None, this a buy and hold Investment.	0.21%
Portfolio 1	Person starting who wants 100% stock market investment. Objective is to match US stock market performance with an index fund.	Migrate to balanced (portfolio 4) near retirement	0.19%
Portfolio 2	Person who wants an 80% US stock and 20% international stock.	Rebalance every year and migrate to balanced (Portfolio 4) near retirement	0.21%
Portfolio 3	Person who seeks high quality and low-cost managed funds that have outperformed the benchmark indices.	Rebalance every year and migrate to balanced (Portfolio 4) near retirement	0.38%
Portfolio 4	Person who wants a balanced portfolio of stocks and bonds.	Annual rebalancing.	0.21%

Each of the investment portfolios is described in more detail below.

Target Retirement Portfolios

The easiest investment strategy for individuals is to purchase mutual funds that automatically change the asset allocation as you near retirement. Vanguard has a target retirement portfolio funds where you simply pick the year that you want to retire. The table below shows the asset allocation for the retirement funds based on the targeted retirement age. Over time each fund will be adjusted to become more conservative. For example in 10 years the 2035 fund will hold the same asset allocation as the 2025 fund. The funds are designed to provide a balanced investment portfolio at retirement age.

Fund Name (retirement year)	Age	Asset Allocation			
		US Stock Market	Foreign Stock	Bonds	Fixed Income
Target Retirement 2005	65	40%	10%	40%	10%
Target Retirement 2010	60	48%	12%	40%	0%
Target Retirement 2015	55	53.3%	13.4%	33.3%	0%
Target Retirement 2020	50	60%	15%	25%	0%
Target Retirement 2025	45	66%	16.5%	17.5%	0%
Target Retirement 2030	40	72%	18%	10%	0%
Target Retirement 2035	35	72%	18%	10%	0%
Target Retirement 2040	30	72%	18%	10%	0%
Target Retirement 2045	25	72%	18%	10%	0%
Target Retirement 2050	20	72%	18%	10%	0%

Portfolio 1: Diversified US Index Fund

The objective of portfolio 1 is to achieve US stock market performance by targeting performance of the overall US stock market with a very low cost index fund. The Vanguard Total Stock Market Index follows the Morgan Stanley Capital International's (MCSI) broad market index. Based on the minimum fund investments, this portfolio is appropriate for account balances between $3,000 and $15,000. This portfolio is appropriate for starting investors.

Portfolio 1: U.S. Market Index

| Portfolio 1 | Fund | Target | 12/31/2007 | Annualized return | | | | Expense |
Fund Name	Symbol	Holding	Fund Price	1	3	5	10	ratio
Total Stock Market Index	VTSMX	100%	$35.36	5.49%	8.90%	13.80%	6.25%	0.19%
			Portfolio Return	5.49%	8.90%	13.80%	6.25%	

Portfolio 2: Diversified US and International Index Funds

The objective of portfolio 2 is to achieve US and international stock market performance by targeting performance of the Wilshire 5000 index (80% holding) and an international index (20% holding). The Total International Stock Index fund invests in European, pacific, and emerging companies. This portfolio is appropriate for accounts greater than or equal to $15,000. This portfolio is ideal for individuals who seek a simple investment strategy that provides excellent diversification and very low fees.

Portfolio 2: 80% US / 20% International Market Index

| Porfolio 2 | Fund | Target | 12/31/2007 | Annualized return | | | | Expense |
Fund Name (Symbol)	Symbol	Holding	Fund Price	1	3	5	10	ratio
Total Stock Market Index	VTSMX	80%	$35.36	5.49%	8.90%	13.80%	6.25%	0.19%
Total International Stock Index	VGTSX	20%	$19.89	15.52%	19.13%	23.45%	9.44%	0.27%
			Portfolio Return	7.50%	10.95%	15.73%	6.89%	0.21%

Portfolio 3: Managed Aggressive Growth Mutual Funds

The objective of portfolio 3 is to invest in multiple managed funds with historical performance greater than the market index. Due to higher required minimum investments, this portfolio is appropriate for portfolios greater than $70,000. This portfolio is good for individuals who seek higher returns than the index and are willing to incur increased risk. This investment approach requires occasional long-term adjustments based on fund performance. The portfolio provides excellent diversification.

Portfolio 3: Managed Funds

Porfolio 3 Fund Name (Symbol)	Fund Symbol	Target Holding	12/31/2007 Fund Price	Annualized return				Expense ratio
				1	3	5	10	
Selected Value	VASVX	40%	$19.29	-0.23%	9.56%	16.44%	8.39%	0.42%
Mid-Cap Index Investor Shares	VIMSX	20%	$20.70	6.02%	11.12%	17.24%		0.22%
Windsor II Investor Growth	VWNFX	20%	$31.26	2.23%	8.96%	14.76%	7.43%	0.33%
Total International Stock Index	VGTSX	20%	$19.89	15.52%	19.13%	23.45%	9.44%	0.27%
			Portfolio Return	**4.66%**	**11.67%**	**17.67%**		**0.33%**

Portfolio 4: Balanced Equity and Bond Funds

The objective of this portfolio is to achieve a balanced portfolio of 50% stock and 50% bonds. This portfolio is targeted to an individual who desires to reduce the risk of losing principal and the objective of achieving returns greater than inflation. This portfolio is designed with index funds. The stock fund portions of this portfolio may be changed to portfolio 3 (above). Individuals may also choose to increase or decrease the percentage of bonds based on risk tolerance. For example, an individual with a pension may reduce the percentage of bonds (since a pension act similar to a bond), while another investor with less risk tolerance may increase bond holdings.

Portfolio 4: Balanced Portfolio

Porfolio 4 Fund Name (Symbol)	Fund Symbol	Target Holding	12/31/2007 Fund Price	Annualized return				Expense ratio
				1	3	5	10	
Total Stock Market Index	VTSMX	40%	$35.36	5.49%	8.90%	13.80%	6.25%	0.19%
Total International Stock Index	VGTSX	10%	$19.89	15.52%	19.13%	23.45%	9.44%	0.27%
Total Bond Index Fund	VBMFX	50%	$10.14	6.92%	4.51%	4.35%	5.71%	0.20%
Portfolio Return				**7.21%**	**7.73%**	**10.04%**	**6.30%**	**0.20%**

Question: Why invest with the Vanguard Group

Question: Many of your recommendations are with Vanguard. Why?

Answer:

There are a handful of quality no-load mutual fund companies. Low cost mutual fund companies to consider include Vanguard, Fidelity, and T Row Price. In writing this publication I want to recommend portfolios that are easy to invest and follow. Many publications recommend portfolios with mutual funds from different mutual fund companies – I find it difficult and impractical to manage a diverse set of funds. In my view there are several factors, which make Vanguard highly appealing.

First, Vanguard's primary purpose is to serve investors with low cost mutual funds as opposed to driving profits. This is evident in that Vanguard was started as a cooperative instead of a corporation. Secondly, Vanguard continues to lower expense ratio fees over time. During the last couple of years Fidelity and Vanguard have been in fierce price competition to provide the lowest cost S&P 500 index fund. During this time the expense ratio for the S&P 500 index fund has dropped in half to less than 0.2% (for larger accounts the fee has dropped to under 0.1%). Contrast these low expense ratios to the mutual fund industry average of 1.35%. Lastly, Vanguard has a solid financial background since 1975.

Part Four

Real Estate and Estate Planning

Financial Steps

1. Define your goals

2. Live within your means

3. Create an emergency fund

4. Eliminate high interest debt

5. Contribute 10% to retirement savings

6. Pay off credit card and consumer debt.

7. Fully fund your rainy day fund

8. Maximize retirement savings contributions

⟹ 9. Continuously build equity and pay off your mortgage

10. Achieve Retirement Security or Financial Independence

Chapter 8
Home Buying and Ownership

A small house can hold as
much happiness as a big one.
–Chinese Proverb

Purchasing and owning a home is a cornerstone of the American Dream. This dream is poignantly captured by a recent quote that I heard from a woman, "My dream is to own a small yellow house with a blue door; every other Sunday I will have my family and friends over for dinner." The fulfillment and benefits of owning a home can be significant. For example, when you own a home, you experience an increase quality of life from both having housing stability and having your own safe retreat from the stresses of life. Buying and owning a home does have its risks and pitfalls though. For example, it's important that you don't overstretch yourself with too much house.

I recommend that you implement the following strategies to maximize your success with buying and owning a home:

1. Be patient and selective in your home choice.
2. Make a significant down payment.
3. Finance with a fixed mortgage.
4. Purchase a home appropriate for your income.
5. Build increasing equity in your house.

Let's review these points one at a time.

Be patient and selective in your home choice.

Most people desire to minimize the frequency of buying and selling houses to minimize both transactions costs (real estate and mortgage fees) and the significant amount of work required to move. I recommend that you treat buying a house as a significant project.

When making any significant purchase it's best to clearly list out your requirements and preferences and take adequate time to make a wise purchase. Clearly defining your purchasing musts and wants will prevent you from buying a house that doesn't meet your needs. List out important factors such as the number of bedrooms, number of bathrooms, single or double story, proximity to your work place, size of garage, and of course price. Then define each factor as a must or a want. If you are married, I recommend that requirements and preferences are listed individually and collectively. Here is an example of criteria from one couple:

Factor	Husband	Wife	Togther
House age	Brand new	1950's	1970's
Bedrooms	3	3	3
Bathrooms	2	2	2
Stories	1 or 2	1	1
Location	In town	In town	in town
Site	Flexible	Quiet	Quiet
Garage	2 car	1 or 2 car	2 car
Miles to work	< 3 miles	< 10 miles	< 5 miles
Heating	Natural Gas	Natural Gas	Natural Gas
Fenced yard	Yes	Yes	Yes

Legend	Must	Want

When you are in the process of buying a house, you will likely experience pressure from both real estate agents and mortgage brokers to proceed quickly. You may hear comments such as, "This house won't last long at this price" or "You should move to lock in these interest rates." This occurs when these people prioritize their interest of making money ahead of your interest of making the right purchase. I recommend that you ignore these pressures and take the time to be confident in your purchasing decision. When my wife and I purchased our house we took nine months to buy. By the time we purchased we knew exactly what we wanted and the fair market value of homes for sale.

Make a significant down payment

We are currently going through a national housing price correction that reminds us that putting no-money-down is a bad strategy. No-money-down mortgages are appealing because the enables people to get into a house, but can be painful when real estate values decline and people need to sell their house. I recommend that you make a 20% down payment on your house. At 20% you do not have to pay mortgage insurance (mortgage insurance is insurance paid by the borrower but provides protection for the lender). Of course, another advantage of paying 20% down is that your mortgage payment is lower. This is important because, many people underestimate increased expenses associated with owning a house. For example, you may need to pay for landscaping your yard, you may purchase furniture, and you may make home improvements.

Finance with a fixed mortgage

Traditionally most mortgages were sold with a fixed interest rate. This means that the interest rate charged (and thus the payment) was the same over the loan period. There has been a dramatic increase in the sale of adjustable rate mortgages. There are a wide variety of adjustable rate mortgage, but the most common ones have a period of time where the interest rate is fixed (five years for example), and then the interest rate changes annually based on the prime interest rate. If you are confident that you will be in a home for only five years, an adjustable rate mortgage may be appropriate. People are attracted to adjustable rate mortgages because the initial low interest rates enable them to purchase a larger house. The dilemma with adjustable rate mortgages is that if interest rates increase then your payments increase accordingly. Given that the majority of people don't get a pay raise when interest rates increase, it's more prudent to buy with a fixed interest rate. I recommend purchasing a house with a 15 or 30 year fixed mortgage. Be sure to compare the costs and rates of a mortgage from three different lenders.

Purchase a home appropriate for your income

Owning a home should bring fulfillment into your life; not increased stress. Banks and mortgage companies evaluate two ratios to determine your maximum mortgage. If you have no debt then the mortgage payment can be 28% of your gross income. The limit of your mortgage payment plus other consumer debts is 36%. For example, for a monthly income of $3000 the maximum mortgage would be $840 per month. If your income is $3000, you have an auto loan for

$250, and a student loan for $200; then the maximum mortgage would be $630. I recommend that you limit your mortgage payment to one-quarter of your take home pay. You will want to have incremental money for retirement savings, building up your rainy day fund, and sustaining a desirable quality of life. Before you purchase a home, mimic making a mortgage payment by saving the difference between your rent and the anticipated mortgage payment.

Build increasing equity in your house

In time, you will likely build equity in your house from the value of your house increasing, from improvements that you make, and from your mortgage principal decreasing in time. I recommend that you resist the temptation to take out home equity loans. I think that it's a good idea to continuously improve your home over time. If you are energetic and skillful you may choose to make many improvements, if you hire professionals then you may initiate an occasional improvement. Home improvements provide an immediate increase in your quality of life. The long-term benefit of making improvements is that you should be able to sell your house easier if necessary. Home improvements typically don't have full immediate payback, thus it's best to limit the amount that is financed by a home equity loan.

Life Application

The next time that you purchase a home: slow down, enjoy the process, and make a great decision for your household. I recommend that you put down 20%, use a fixed interest rate mortgage, and limit your mortgage payment to 20% of your take home income. Once you own a home, continuously build equity by both avoiding equity loans and continuously improving and updating your home.

Challenge for home buying and ownership:

Get your estate plan in order:
- Be patient and selective in your home choice.
- Make a significant down payment.
- Finance with a fixed mortgage.
- Purchase a home appropriate for your income.
- Build increasing equity in your house.

Chapter 9
Complete your Estate Plan

We make a living by what we get,
but we make a life by what we give.
–Winston Churchill

While few of us want to think about the possibility of dying, none of us want to consider dying without a solid estate plan. Imagine the fate of your children, pets, and wealth being decided by the courts. According to the US government, half of Americans die without completing a will. My challenge to you is for you to either start or improve your estate plan.

Here are the essentials to establishing a solid estate plan:

1. Carry adequate life insurance for your survivors
2. Update your beneficiary information on your retirement and investment accounts.
3. Compete a will
4. Complete a medical directive and assign your healthcare proxy
5. Give while you are alive.

Let's review these points one at a time.

Carry adequate life insurance for your survivors.

Inadequate life insurance is one of the most unfortunate scenarios for a surviving family. Not only do the survivors have to grieve the loss of a loved-one, but also face the long-term financial stress of making ends meet. It's important to have the right amount of life insurance, the right type of life insurance, and to shop competitively.

Determine the amount of required life insurance by considering the money needed to pay off the house, pay for childcare, pay for college education, and replace missed wages. A general guideline is to buy 10 times your annual income. This would mean that a person earning $50,000 per year would consider a $500,000 term policy. Also recognize that a life insurance policy on a non-working spouse makes sense to provide for care of children. The bottom line question is, how much money would the family need if there is an unexpected death of a parent? If nobody is dependent on your income then life insurance is not needed.

I recommend the purchase of level term life insurance. Level term life insurance means that the death benefit remains the same during the life of the policy. A 40-year non-smoker male can purchase 20-year level policy with a $500,000 life insurance benefit for about $450 per year. The actual price will change with age, health, and the number of policy years. Avoid whole life insurance products that combine life insurance with investments. Whole life investment insurance is very expensive and aggressively sold by sales people seeking large commissions. Better to buy level term life insurance and do your own investing. Recognize that you won't need life insurance once you achieve retirement security or financial independence. Good places to start your search for term life insurance are Insure.com and termassistant.com. These companies competitively shop among life insurance companies for you. Make sure to purchase from a life insurance company that is rated A or higher.

Update your beneficiary information in your retirement accounts.

Did you know that your beneficiary designations in your retirement accounts (401K, 403b, IRA, pension, etc) take priority over the wishes of your will? It's therefore important to review and update your beneficiary information annually. Updating beneficiary information is quite easy today, especially with online accounts. I recommend that you take 30 minutes today and review your beneficiary designations.

Complete a will.

What happens if I don't complete a will? The courts will appoint an executor who will assign guardianship for your children and distribute your wealth within the limits of the law. Therefore the most important reason to complete a will is to insure that your wishes are executed in a timely manner. Here are examples of important instructions that you can have within a will.

- Naming an executor who will carry out your wishes.

- Naming a guardian to care for your children

- Instructions for distribution of wealth and possessions.

- Instructions for care of your pets.

I recommend a two-step process to setup your will. First complete a will (one for each spouse if married) on your own using an Internet site or standardized legal forms. Completing a will online is easy and quick – the most difficult part is making decisions about your wishes. This will save you money since you will not be paying an attorney by the hour to ask you questions. In my search for a simple and inexpensive online will, I discovered Build AWill. Their process is intuitive and you can complete a will for any state for under $30. Once your will is complete, then have it reviewed by an attorney to both insure that you aren't missing something significant and to insure that it's legally binding.

You may also consider setting up a trust if you have significant wealth, have a complicated situation such as a blended family, or want to avoid the risk that your will may be challenged. A trust can't be challenged as it avoids the court probate process. A trust is best created and maintained with the services of an attorney.

As you can imagine it's important that a copy of your will is assessable to your attorney (if applicable), your executor, and other close family. It's also a good idea to review your wishes with your executor to further insure your wishes are carried out.

Complete an advanced directive and identify your healthcare proxy

In addition to your financial wishes, it's important that your medical wishes are followed. This is best done by completing an advanced directive and naming your healthcare proxy.

You can obtain an advanced directive application at the National Hospice and Palliative Care Organization (NHPCO) at http://www.nhpco.org/. After you have completed the forms it's important provide a copy to your physician, spouse, close family, and friends. Also review your advanced directive with the person who you assign as your healthcare proxy.

It's advisable to assign a healthcare proxy. This is also known as your durable medical power of attorney. Use a durable medical power of attorney form to identify the person who will make medical choices for you in the event that you cannot.

Give while you are alive

Giving while you are alive is great way to insure that your wishes are fulfilled. You may also choose to invest in your family legacy by investing in education for your children or grandchildren, contributing to your favorite charities, or creating memories for your heirs by taking them on a vacation.

One key advantage of giving while you are alive is that you can see firsthand the benefits. Additionally you can adopt and modify your giving based on the results that you observe.

Life Application

Now is the time to start or improve you estate plan. Completing an estate plan will give you the peace of mind knowing that your wishes will be followed.

> ## Life Application:
>
> Get your estate plan in order:
> 1. Carry adequate life insurance for your survivors
> 2. Update your beneficiary information on your retirement and investment accounts.
> 3. Compete a will (or setup a trust)
> 4. Complete a medical directive and assign your healthcare proxy
> 5. Give while you are alive.

About the Author

Rio Rivas lives in the Pacific Northwest. He has taken economic courses at both Stanford and Lehigh University. He has Masters Of Technology from National Technical University. He works as an engineer for a Fortune 500 technology company. Rio is an inventor on 6 patents. He enjoys hiking with his wife and dogs. Investing and helping others with personal finance have been long-term rewarding interests.

Follow your dreams, and achieve your goals!
-Rio

Please visit the author's web site at www.riorivas.com for a complimentary articles and book resources.

Send your success stories, feedback, and corrections to riorivas@peak.org.